FISHING FOR FUN—

And To Wash Your Soul

FISHING
FOR FUN–

And
To Wash Your Soul

HERBERT HOOVER

Edited by William Nichols

RANDOM HOUSE
New York

This little book of meditations is dedicated to

FISHERMEN

FISHERLADIES

FISHER YOUNGSTERS

They, at times, escape—or cast off—the tram-
mels of life into a land of enchantment. Perhaps
this will extend the moments in that land of
joys and illusions.

The pleasant'st angling is to see the fish
Cut with her golden oars the silver stream,
And greedily devour the treacherous bait.

SHAKESPEARE

Preface

There is no subtle reason for this little book. Over many years in meetings of fishermen and fisherwomen, in public addresses, and in articles for magazines, I have made observations on fishing.

Along came a publisher, who said to me: "These meditations would make a little book of good cheer. And in the daily grind of trying to find out why the Communists get that way, it would be an expedition into relief." So here they are. I have made no changes in the original texts except for occasional editing and condensation.

Herbert Hoover

Foreword

Fishing is a chance to wash one's soul with pure air, with the rush of the brook, or with the shimmer of the sun on the blue water.

It brings meekness and inspiration from the scenery of nature, charity toward tackle makers, patience toward fish, a mockery of profits and egos, a quieting of hate, a rejoicing that you do not have to decide a darned thing until next week.

And it is discipline in the equality of man —for all men are equal before fish.

Subjects

FISHING FOR FUN—

And To Wash Your Soul

The Reasons Why
They Get That Way

The reason for it all is that fishing is fun and good for the soul of man.

The human animal originally came from out-of-doors. When spring begins to move in his bones, he just must get out again. Moreover, as civilization, cement pavements, office buildings, and radios have overwhelmed us, the need for regeneration has increased, and the

[*17*]

impulses are even stronger. When all the routines and details and the human bores get on our nerves, we just yearn to go away from here to somewhere else.

When you get full up of telephone bells, church bells, office boys, columnists, pieces of paper and the household chores—you get that urge to go away from here. Going fishing is the only explanation in the world that even skeptics will accept.

Nor is it the fish we get that count. We could buy them in the market for mere silver at one percent of the cost. Fishing is much more than fish; it is the vitalizing lure to outdoor life. It is the great occasion when we may return to the fine simplicity of our forefathers.

And there is the chance to associate with fishermen. You have the opportunity to renew old and long-time friendships. All fishermen and fisherladies are by nature friendly and righteous persons. No one of them ever went to jail while fishing—unless they forgot to buy a license.

I need not extol to you the joys of outdoor life, its values in relaxation, its contribution to real and successful work. The spiritual uplift of the good will, cheerfulness and optimism that accompanies every fishing expedition is the particular spirit that our people need in these troublous times of suspicion and doubt.

Life is not comprised entirely of making a living or of arguing about the future or defaming the past. It is the break of the waves in the sun, the contemplation of the eternal flow of the stream, the stretch of forest and mountain in their manifestation of the Maker—it is all these that soothe our troubles, shame our wickedness, and inspire us to esteem our fellow men—especially other fishermen.

Strong primary instincts—and they are useful instincts—get rejuvenation by a thrust into the simpler life. For instance, we do not catch fish in the presence of, or by the methods of, our vast complex of industrialism, nor in the luxury of summer hotels, nor through higher thought, for that matter. In our outdoor life we get repose from the troubles of soul that this vast complex of civilization imposes upon us in our working hours and our restless nights. Association with the placid ripples of the waves and the quiet chortle of the streams is soothing to our "het-up" anxieties.

I am for fishing for fun as a contribution to constructive joy because it gives an excuse and an impulse to take to the woods and to the water. Moreover, fishing has democratic values because the same privilege of joy is open to the country boy as to the city lad. (And equally to his properly brought-up city or farmer dad.)

Lots of people committed crimes during the year who would not have done so if they had been fishing. The increase of crime is among those deprived of the regenerations that impregnate the mind and character of fishermen.

Our standards of material progress include the notion and the hope that we shall lessen the daily hours of labor on the farm, at the bench, and in the office. We also dream of longer annual holidays and more of them, as scientific discovery and mass production do our production job faster and faster. But they dull the souls of men. Even now, the great majority of us really work no more than eight hours a day. And if we sleep eight hours we have eight hours in which to ruminate and make merry or stir the caldron of evil. This civilization is not going to depend upon what we do when we work so much as what we do in our time off.

The moral and spiritual forces of our country do not lose ground in the hours we are busy on our jobs; their battle is the leisure time. We associate joy with leisure. We have great machinery for joy, some of it destructive, some of it synthetic, some of it mass production. We go to chain theaters and movies; we watch somebody else knock a ball over the fence or kick it over the goal post. I do that too and I believe in it. I do, however, insist that no organized joy has values comparable to the outdoors. . . . We gain none of the rejuvenating cheer that comes from return to the solemnity, the calm and inspiration of primitive nature.

Contemplation of the eternal flow of the stream, the stretch of forest and mountain, all reduce our egotism, soothe our troubles, and

shame our wickedness. And in it we make a physical effort that no sitting on cushions, benches, or side lines provides. To induce people to take this joy they need some stimulant from the hunt, the fish or the climb. I am for fish.

Izaak Walton
on Fishing for Fun

Three hundred and nine years ago, Izaak Walton published the first book on the beatitudes of fishing, entitled *The Compleat Angler or, the Contemplative Man's Reaction*. His attitude toward the beatitudes of fishing needs little explanation beyond the title, and at one point he remarks: "God never did make a more calm, quiet, innocent recreation than angling." Izaak fished with worms and artificial flies, all of which he explains in great detail.

The fishing beatitudes are much amplified since Izaak's times. He lived in a simpler world, and did not spend the major part of his life answering a bell. He never got the jumps from traffic signals or the price of wheat. But Izaak was a milliner by trade and, though he was not driven into the wilds by these noises, yet the daily association with women's hats probably effected the same result in him. And he might have learned how to tie and make artificial flies through making hats; especially as he had to deal with feathers.

Every fisherman has his favorite quotations from Izaak Walton. One of mine is: *We may say of angling, as Dr. Boteler said of strawberries: "Doubtless God could have made a better berry, but doubtless God never did"; and so, if I might be judge, God never did make a more calm, quiet, innocent recreation than angling.*

Where Ponce de León
Lost the Fountain of Youth

Every school child knows that about 450 years ago Ponce de León came to Florida in search of the waters of the Fountain of Youth. In his journeys he missed Lake Okeechobee by only about forty miles. I can tell you that he could have found a veritable fountain of youth. There are fish hereabouts. And fishing is the eternal Fountain of Youth.

For your assurance of this fact, I will men–

tion that there is said to be a tablet of 2000 B.C. which says:

> *The Gods do not subtract from the allotted span of men's lives the hours spent in fishing.*

As further proof that fishing is the Fountain of Youth, I may also cite that many a President of the United States has sought the Fountain of Youth by fishing. . . . Also, fishing reduces the ego in Presidents and former Presidents, for at fishing most men are not equal to boys.

The Gigantic Army
of Game Fishermen

More people have gone fishing over more centuries than for any other human recreation.

Man and boy, the American is a fisherman. The Declaration of Independence is firm that all men—and boys—are endowed with unalienable rights, which obviously include the pursuit of fish. America is a well-watered country, and the inhabitants know all of the fishing holes.

Based upon the number of fishing licenses issued in licensing states, the Bureau of Fisheries estimates that less than one million Americans went game fishing in 1906. Now more than twenty-five million persons pay for licenses each year, and veterans and children mostly go for free. The whole Allied world never had that number of men in armies at the same time.

I have no sympathy with attempts at disarmament of the gigantic army which every year marches against the fish. Nor am I for any limitations on its equipment of automobiles, tackle, or incantations. Peace on earth will not come that way. I am for more fish.

The Mentality
of Fishermen

Fishing is not so much getting fish as it is a state of mind and a lure for the human soul into refreshment.

A fisherman must be of contemplative mind, for it is often a long time between bites. Those interregnums emanate patience, reserve, and calm reflection—for no one can catch fish

in anger, or in malice. He is by nature an opti-
mist or he would not go fishing; for we are
always going to have better luck in a few min-
utes or tomorrow. All of which creates a spirit
of affection for fellow fishermen and high
esteem for fishing.

The spiritual uplift of good will, cheerfulness and optimism that accompanies every fishing expedition is the peculiar spirit that our
people need in these troublous times of suspicion and doubt. They ought all to be sent fishing
periodically.

A good fisherman possesses much faith and
hope or he would not fish. He gains even in
charity when he listens to other fishermen.

War, murrain, famine, pestilence, dicta-
tors, the rise and fall of empires or republics
may defeat the game fisherman temporarily,
but he always rises again to invade the streams
and the sea.

[31]

Fishermen are gregarious. Otherwise, the mighty deeds of the day or of a year ago or of ten years ago would go unsung. No one but fishermen will listen to them. Therefore, as two or three are gathered together, the spiritual vitamins of faith, hope and charity have constant regeneration. And we need all in these years of creaking civilization.

There are certain myths about fish that people generally believe. Every fisherman is always astonished at the miracles in fishing that happen to him and he holds to incantations. All American small boys spit on the bait.

There is a particular belief that goes among most fishermen and that is that they have a divine right to unlimited fish. They have inherited this notion from ten thousand generations of free fishermen.

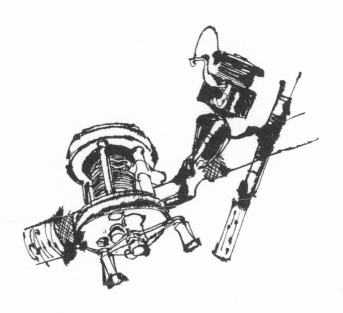

The Class Distinction among Fishermen

Although all men are equal before fish, there are some class distinctions among them. The dry-fly devotees hold themselves a bit superior to the wet-fly fishermen; the wet-fly fishermen, superior to the spinner fishermen; and the spinners, superior to the bait fishermen. I have noticed, however, that toward the end of the day when there are no strikes, each social level collapses in turn down the scale until it gets some fish for supper.

The swordfish and tarpon fishermen also have some social distinctions on the basis of the size of line and reel. The lower-thread line operators are the dukes and earls in that aristocracy. The swordfish and marlin devotees are naturally superior to those who take mere mackerel, amberjacks or flounders. The bonefish fishermen claim a little superiority to the tarpon seekers. But it is not economic status that counts in such good society so much as knowing what the fish bite.

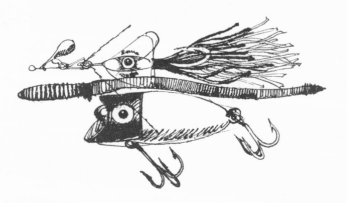

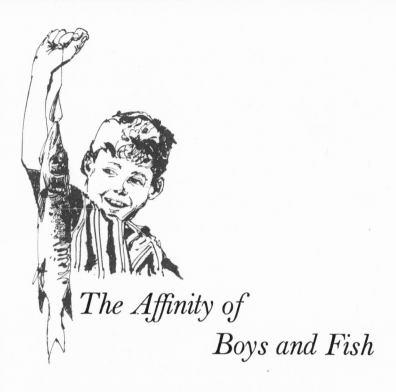

The Affinity of
Boys and Fish

Every true fisherman must have an affection for his neighbors, and especially for the barefoot boy whence we all started our fishing careers.

I was a boy in the days before our civilization became so perfect, before it was paved with cement and made of bricks. Boys were not so largely separated from Mother Earth and all her works. And that was before the machine

[35]

age denied them their natural right as primitive, combative animals to match their wits with birds and animals.

The most vivid and joyous recollections of my Iowa boyhood days are of patient angling in Iowa streams for the very occasional fish, with a willow pole and a properly spat-upon worm.

No royal gourmet has ever provided me with game of such wondrous flavor as fish or birds cooked over a small boy's campfire; pigeons from Iowa's woods and prairie chickens from her hedges, hunted down by our gang with homemade bows and arrows, and slingshots.

One time, in the spring, our grandmothers used to give us nasty brews from sulphur and herbs to purify our blood of the winter's corruptions. They knew something was the matter with the boys. They could have saved trouble by giving them a pole, a string and a hook. Some wise ones—among them my own—did just that.

I have been possessed with the notion that the joys of boyhood, the strengthening of vision, curiosity and patience in his mind, can have no greater contribution than just free fishing. And these qualities are badly needed as armies of boys march into national life year by year.

When I was ten years old, I was transported to Oregon. Oregon lives in my mind for its gleaming wheat fields, its abundant fruit, its luxuriant forest vegetation, and the fish in

the mountain streams. To step into its forests with their tangles of berry bushes, their ferns, their masses of wild flowers, stirs up odors peculiar to Oregon. Within these woods are never-ending journeys of discovery, and the hunts for grouse and expeditions for trout.

There was not so much water in proportion to the fish then, and legal limits had not been thought of. I, like other boys, fished with worms until a generous fisherman, whom we met during an excursion to the upper Santiam, gave four of us three artificial flies each. They proved powerfully productive. It never occurred to me that they were perishable. In any event, I nursed those three flies and used them until all the feathers were worn off—and still the trout rose to them. The upper Santiam has sadly degenerated since. A brand-new fly of

any variety, even when carefully treated with cosmetics and attached to gut leaders and expensive rods, has nothing like the potency of that bamboo pole and the fly tied directly upon the end of a string. (To a boy, climbing out of a thousand-foot-deep canyon was an evening's task of no effort at all in those days.)

The Boy Scout movement has opened for boys the portals to adventure and constructive joy—by reviving the lore of the frontier and the campfire; by establishing contacts with the birds and sometimes with the bees; by matching their patience to the deliberative character of fish; by efficient operation of the swimming hole, and by peeps into the thousand mysteries of the streams, and the trees, and the stars. . . .

The Equipment of
This Army of Fishermen

We have indeed made stupendous progress in
physical equipment to overcome the mysteries
of fish. We have moved upward from the rude
social level of the willow pole with a butcher-
string line, fixed with hooks ten for a dime,
whose compelling lure was one segment of an
angleworm and whose incantation was spitting
on the bait.

Now we have arrived at the high state of a tackle assembled from the steel of Damascus, the bamboos of Siam, the silk of Japan, the lacquer of China, the tin of Bangkok, the nickel of Canada, the feathers of Brazil, and the silver of Colorado—all compounded by mass production at Chicago, Illinois, and Akron, Ohio. And for magic and incantations we have progressed to application of cosmetics to artificial flies; and to wonders in special clothing with pigeonholes for varied lures and liniments, and to calling a bite a "strike." Fishing is not the rich man's sport, though his incantations are more expensive. And I ask you, in the face of all this overwhelming equipment and progress, is there any less time between bites?

However, our fishermen can put in many joyous hours at home polishing up the rods, reels and lures, and deciding on new flies when the imponderable forces of spring begin to move their bones. They could not get such joy out of a collection of live angleworms, and that is all a part of what we are trying to get at anyway—recreation and soul satisfaction.

The Time between Bites of Stream Fish Grows Longer and Longer

Americans produce millions of automobiles. These coördinated forces of inalienable right— the automobile and the call of the fishing hole— propel the man and boy and his mother and sister to search all the available water. This army of fishermen has overworked most of the fishing holes, and the time between bites has become longer and longer, and the fish have become wiser and wiser.

Despite the statistical efficiency of our Department of Commerce, I do not know how many fish each one of the army captured last year. Judging by my own experience, the fishing was not so good. I spent several days searching fishing holes at various points between Chesapeake Bay and the Pacific; I tried to find some spot where not more than six automobiles had already camped, or where the campers did not get up before daylight and thus get the two or three fish which were off guard at that time of day.

The State of New Jersey secures an accounting from its licensees of the number of game fish they catch. It works out at about 4.5 fish per fisherman per annum. Therefore, I conclude that even in that well-organized state it was heavy going.

I submit to you that each fisherman ought to catch at least fifty during the season. I would like more than that myself, but that figure ought to be demanded as a minimum under the "rights" as implied in the Declaration, provided it included one big one for purpose of indelible memory and conversation.

There will be no joy on long winter nights making reinventory of the tackle unless there be behind it the indelible recollection of having caught a few big ones, and the anticipation of bigger ones to come.

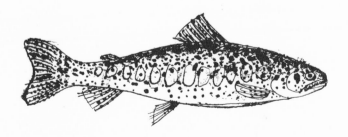

The Bringing-Up
of Infant Fish

Nearly ninety years ago game fishermen began to complain bitterly to their Congressmen about the expanding time between bites, which in economic terms is called the "lag." As an equal opportunity for fishing must be properly considered by any great government as a necessity to public tranquillity, measures were at once taken. The great government said, "We will now apply artificial means to the natural birth and distribution of fish."

The federal government, state governments, and local fishing clubs built hundreds of hatcheries for stream and sea-going fish. In these mass-production works, the maternal carelessness of laying eggs loose in the water to be eaten by cannibalistic relatives and friends was to be halted. The eggs were thereafter carefully safeguarded in glass jars and troughs at controlled temperatures. The baby fingerlings thus born in security and reared in comfort to half an inch long were then distributed back to the streams, being thereupon started on their happy way to be eaten by the same relatives as fresh meat instead of fresh eggs.

During the last few years, hundreds of hatcheries, working on fifteen species of game fish, turned out an average of one billion infant game fish to be duly launched into life among

the cannibals. In addition to these paternalistic
and maternal endeavors, private enterprise in
the shape of responsible mother fish has been
working upon the same problem; they are
probably doing more than paternal government, for all I know. Private enterprise usually
does.

I may say parenthetically that I introduce
my estimate of birth registration and infant
mortality among fish because it will relieve
your minds of anxiety as to the future. But if
anyone feels these figures may be wrong, he
has my permission to divide or multiply them
by any factor based upon his own experience.

Still we must face the solemn fact that only
some microscopic percent of these fry or fingerlings, whether synthetic or natural, ever live to
that state of grandeur which will serve as an
inspiration to polish the tackle or insure the ap-
proach to the battle in renewed hope with each
oncoming season. And we lose ground every

year, sector by sector, as the highways include
more fishing holes in their routes.

The automobile with its easy transit to all
fishing centers and the growing spread of fishing as a stimulus to outdoor life make it neces-
sary that we inaugurate new policies. If we do
not we shall see our greatest national instructor
of the calm and contemplative mind fail right
in the middle of a most hectic civilization.

Pollution

Aside from the cannibalistic enemies of infant, adolescent, and adult fish, acting in lively alliance with the organized army of twenty-five million fishermen, we have still another fish enemy to deal with. That is pollution. Herein is the poison cup which we give to eggs, fry, fingerlings, adolescents, and adult fish alike.

Now, if we want fish we have to reserve some place for them to live. They only occur in the water, but it happens that nature adapted them to clean water. I suppose that was because nature foresaw no fishing beatitudes along a sewer.

This question of pollution has a multitude of complications. There are as many opinions about pollution as there are minds concerning it. Pollution exists in different waters in different degrees, from ships, factories, coal mines, chemical works in cities and towns—to mention only a few of them. Many of these things damage public health, destroy the outdoor appeal of the streams, and all of them damage the fish.

But after all we are an industrial people. We have to work eight hours a day and all but a few weeks in the year, and we cannot abolish our industries and still pay for fishing tackle. So I have long since come to the conclusion that what we really need in every state, through our state authorities, is a survey of all the streams and a division of them into three categories.

The *first* task is to determine the streams that have not yet been polluted, then give immediate protection to these streams, or parts of them, that they never shall be polluted; that no industry shall be allowed to settle upon them unless there is adequate guarantee that there will be no pollution.

The *second* category includes the streams that are polluted to the finish. There are many of these that could never be recovered, as a matter of practical fact, without the displacement of hundreds of thousands of people from their homes through the crushing of their industries. The numbers who would benefit by clearing them would be infinitesimal compared to the suffering and loss implied in such an operation.

Then we should have a *third* category of streams—those that are perhaps partially polluted, where we could get correction by systematic and sound action and gradually restore them to the first category.

The Hardships
of Stream Fishing

For years I have recommended fishing as the remedy for all moral, spiritual, and physical ills. Perhaps I should show a balanced mind by a frank statement of the cruel hardships when fishing. The amount of hardship varies with the kind of fish you are after.

There are two handicaps which apply to all expeditions for fish. The first is the depletion of your savings. You must buy more tackle; and you must bring one coat with large checks.

Passers-by will then know you are a real sport. You can wear your old pants. You must also buy a canvas jacket with seventeen pockets to carry the gadgets and bottles for emergencies. The second hardship relates to frustration. You have been dreaming for the previous six months about that big one. But your appointment with destiny will connect you with the smaller sizes.

To fish in streams and lakes, you go away from your own comfortable food supply and bed. Having engaged this new habitation in advance, you arrive to find the cook has usually just resigned or gives you a boiled egg which should have been scrambled with mustard. Your coffee is part of that used in days gone by. There is always a loose spring in the bed. If the food is good, you eat too much.

In order to prevent your getting a big one, some states require you to throw back any fish over fourteen inches.

There are signs every half-mile warning

you of thirty days in jail. Also about this time, you look up at the bank and see a sign on a tree: PRIVATE PROPERTY—NO FISHING. Your comment becomes worse than that for which your mother washed your mouth with soap.

If you are fishing for trout, you can do it either from the bank or mid-stream or at prohibitive expense from a boat. In casting a fly from the bank, you spend alternate half-hours climbing trees trying to get your fly and leader back. Most times you don't get them, even with the beguilement of words. If you are fishing mid-stream, you must have those special waterproof pants which reach from inside hobnailed shoes to your armpits. You must carry

an iron-pointed staff to prevent your being washed downstream. When that happens, the waterproof pants fill with water and you sink. If you have the good sense to hold onto the iron-pointed staff, you possibly save your life. But you will need to buy a new rod and reel. Also, when attired in this mid-stream apparatus, you will find your fly is not the right one.

To brace yourself with the iron-pointed staff and at the same time change the fly, you must tuck your rod under your armpit and change the fly with one hand and your teeth. That fly is also usually the wrong one.

When you do not get anything on a dry fly, you descend to a wet one. As that fails, you begin to think about the need of fish for dinner and to show the other guests at the auto camp. Then you try hardware of different sorts. Failing with these, you take on the cans of salmon eggs or worms that you have hidden in your secret pockets. This has long been classified TOP SECRET. Incidentally, when it really rains, your sport is playing solitaire on your bedroom bureau.

There is also stream fishing for salmon. The really aristocratic spots are in Eastern Canada. That variety has two griefs. You must not only buy special clothes, but you must engage an Indian and his canoe. He charges you separately for these two parts of equipment. And of course you pay a rate for board and lodging, which includes the hire of the total staff during the long winter.

The provincial government charges you about five hundred dollars for the season's use of a half-mile of one of their rivers. In the end you may get a big one, but the average expense is about one thousand dollars per fish. You can get one of equal weight, although a little less flavor, at a California market for less than five dollars.

The Hardships
of Salt-Water Fishing

Your ambition being to get a six- or ten-foot sailfish or swordfish, or an oversized tuna or dolphin, you go to the neighborhood of the Gulf Stream, the Humboldt Stream or Japanese Stream. If you buy your own tackle and its spare parts with which to wear such monsters into subjection, you will need to negotiate a long-time loan of great magnitude. You may think your physical improvement will save on doctor's bills later. But not so. You will need special treatments when you get home.

Also, you must hire a good-size motorboat with a crew of at least two. Their gaze at you is always clouded with pity. And if they furnish the tackle, the charter money would hire an

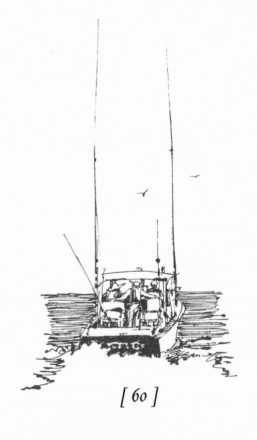

oil tanker. Also, these boats have a habit of suddenly descending to the floor of the sea, then rising up to the sky in a fashion that takes your breakfast overboard. You spend the whole day hanging onto the boat with your right hand, and with your left hand dragging a dead fish in the far-away behind the boat.

But if you are lucky enough to get one of these sea monsters on your line, you spend the next hour cranking the reel with a special spinal motion called pumping. About the time you get him alongside, a shark bites him in two pieces and keeps the larger half. Or the boatman misses him with the gaff. If you are also a stream fisherman, you already have restrained language at hand.

I have withheld mention of mosquitoes and black flies, since they are applicable to all kinds of fishing. Their distribution in the Western Hemisphere is one of the wonders of nature. If you have a fish on the line, then the fly bites. Slapping at the fly on your face is one of the methods for unhooking the fish.

As part of your seagoing equipment you must take several varieties of liniment and sunburn dope. You will need periodical libations of the liniment on your muscles all night long. Sunburn is a serious business. Each of your friends has a sure preventive dope. Do not be fooled—the sun is used to all of them. The only real protection is a burglar's mask or a skin-diving suit. In case you go home during the early stages of sunburn, the first kid you meet will tell you that you have need for a new face.

Bonefishing

There are some kinds of sea fishing especially adapted to your elder years. There is the bonefish. You pursue him on the flats of the Florida Keys at high tide in a skiff, sitting on a two-cushioned chair. You hire a guide to do all the work of pushing the boat about, and he will tell you of the superior skill of his last customer. You have much time between bites to contemplate—or to read long Government reports. This shallow water is also proof against stomach upheavals.

You have to hunt for a bonefish, and when you find signs of where he is, you cast him a shrimp. At times, our bonefish is digging for a hermit crab for himself. Then his tail sticks out of the water and he wags it at you. Most times he is not eating shrimp that day. Other days the water is too cold or the tide runs out, or the bonefish has just stayed home. This is good training in restrained thinking.

On Stuffing Fish for
Household Ornaments —
for Proof of Prowess

On those rare occasions during deep-sea fishing
when you get a monster on board, your first
thought is to perpetuate your triumph and
convince your wife you caught him. The first
step to evidence is to have him weighed by the
wharfkeeper and get a written certificate. It is
useful to give the wharfkeeper a tip. The second
step of evidence for your wife is to have him
stuffed. This is also the way to demonstrate to

all persons your great triumph. That costs $175 per fish, paid in advance.

After he is stuffed and you have paid the bill and the freight and truck charges, you must mount him over the living-room mantel, where you hope he will provide a conversational item, and that all your guests will marvel. You can gently blend in your great skill, courage and endurance. The neighbors only come once.

By and by your wife disapproves of him as a household ornament and insists he has moths. Anyway, she bribes the garbage man with five dollars to take him away while you are at the office.

If you are inclined toward having your fish stuffed, I suggest you wait until you can observe the rubbish barges going to the dump at sea. You can see them in the early morning at the piers. And you will find them topped with stuffed fish. The barge man will accommodate you with one for a dollar or less—and throw in for free the moths and weevils.

One man of my acquaintance saved his stuffed sailfish from his wife's zeal by digging a hole in the floor of his library—put his sailfish in it and bolted a plate glass over it. He put a lamp in the fish's eye and could wink it with a secret button. His guests expressed astonishment. With this conversational springboard, he was able to recite the history of each sailfish he had caught. His wife always remained silent.

Fishing Presidents
and Candidates

There are a dozen justifications for fishing.
Among them is its importance to the political
world. No political aspirant can qualify for
election unless he demonstrates he is a fisherman, there being twenty-five million persons
who pay annually for a license to fish.

In Roman times the people formed their

political auguries by observing the flights of birds and the entrails of dead sheep. I have recently been fishing. In the long time between bites I have come to the firm conclusion that today fish take the place of the flight of birds and the entrails of sheep.

Also, I should inform you that from an augury point of view, there are two kinds of fish: There are the host of species of common or garden fish which are the recreation of the common man. There are also the rare species of fish sought by the aristocracy of fishermen. They require more equipment and more incantations than merely spitting on the bait. Politically speaking, these fish can be ignored since they are only landed the hard way and have no appeal to most voters.

A few years ago a press photograph showed my friend, the late Senator Taft, awkwardly holding a common fish. It was taken from many angles for all the common men to see. I knew without other evidence that he was a candidate. Some years ago my friend, General Eisenhower, burst into photographs from all angles, gingerly holding three very common fish. The augury was positive.

The political potency of fish is known to Presidents as well as candidates. In modern times all Presidents quickly begin to fish soon after election. I am told that McKinley, Taft, Wilson and Harding all undertook fishing in a tentative way, but for the common fishes.

President Coolidge apparently had not fished before election. Being a fundamentalist in religion, economics and fishing, he began his fish career for common trout with worms. Ten million fly fishermen at once evidenced disturbed minds. Then Mr. Coolidge took to a fly. He gave the Secret Service guards great excitement in dodging his backcast and rescuing flies from trees. There were many photographs. Soon after that he declared he did not choose to run again.

President Franklin Roosevelt caught many common fish from the military base of a battleship.

President Truman, prior to his 1948 election, appeared once in a photograph somewhere in a boat gingerly holding a common fish in his arms. An unkind reporter wrote that someone else had caught it. I can find no trace of the letter that the reporter must have received. It is also reported that Mr. Truman was fishing somewhere north of Key West when his boat was surrounded by sharks. But sharks are always a bad augury. Mr. Truman did not run for a third term.

President Theodore Roosevelt, President Cleveland and myself—with a slight egotism!—I think, are the only Presidents who had been lifelong fly fishermen before they went to the White House.

Everyone knows of the first Roosevelt
that he was a valiant hunter of big animals, and
generally an evangel of the strenuous life—
which included fishing. He relates an adventure with an Adirondack stream when he was
twelve years old:

"After dinner all of us began to 'whip'
the rapids. At first I sat on a rock by
the water but the black flies drove me
from there, so I attempted to cross the
rapids. But I had miscalculated my
strength for before I was half way
across the force of the current had

swept me into water which was above my head. Leaving the pole to take [care] of itself I struck out for a rock. My pole soon stuck and so I recovered it. I then went half wading, half swimming down stream, fishing all the time but unsuccessful."

President Cleveland is author of a delightful little volume called *Fishing and Hunting Sketches*, in which he sets forth his ideas on the beatitudes of those sports. As a fisherman, he preferred small-mouthed black bass to trout, and in this respect claimed kinship to another political fisherman, Daniel Webster, from whose history he draws this interesting example of the interrelation of fishing and politics:

"Perhaps," writes President Cleveland, "none of Mr. Webster's orations were more notable or added more to his lasting fame than that delivered at the laying of the cornerstone of the Bunker Hill monument, and it will probably be conceded that its most impressive and beautiful passage was addressed to the survivors of the war for independence then present, beginning with the words 'Venerable Men.'

"This thrilling oratorical flight was composed and elaborated by Mr. Webster while wading waist deep and casting his flies in Mashapee waters. He himself afterwards often referred to this circumstance; and one who was his companion on this particular occasion has recorded the fact that, noticing indications of laxity in fishing action on Mr. Webster's part, he approached him, and that, in the exact words of this witness, 'he seemed to be gazing at the overhanging trees, and presently, advancing one foot and extending his right hand, he commenced to speak—*Venerable Men...*'"

Mr. Cleveland says that he got this story from Webster's guide, who told him that the Massachusetts Senator frequently prepared his orations in this wise, and was in the habit of addressing "mighty strong and fine talk to the fish."

President Cleveland adds, "It is impossible to avoid the conclusion that the fishing habit, by promoting close association with nature, by teaching patience and by generating or stimulating useful contemplation, tends directly to the increase of the intellectual power of its votaries and through them to the improvement of our national character."

That Presidents have taken to fishing in an astonishing fashion seems to me worthy of investigation. I think I have discovered the reason: it is the silent sport. One of the few opportunities given a President for the refreshment of his soul and the clarification of his thoughts by solitude lies through fishing. As I have said in another place, it is generally realized and accepted that prayer is the most personal of all human relationships. Everyone knows that on such occasions men and women are entitled to be alone and undisturbed.

Next to prayer, fishing is the most personal relationship of man; and of more importance, everyone concedes that the fish will not bite in the presence of the public, including newspapermen.

Fishing seems to be one of the few avenues left to Presidents through which they may escape to their own thoughts, may live in their own imaginings, find relief from the pneumatic hammer of constant personal contacts, and refreshment of mind in rippling waters. Moreover, it is a constant reminder of the democracy

of life, of humility and of human frailty. It is
desirable that the President of the United
States should be periodically reminded of this
fundamental fact—that the forces of nature
discriminate for no man.

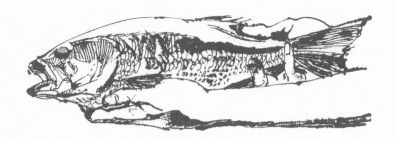

*I may offer two fishermen's tales which came
to me while President.*

An Adventure in Salmon

Each year for many years before I came to the
White House, the directors of a fishing club
personally brought their first salmon of the
season to the White House for the President.
Each time they were duly photographed with
the President and the fish. These photographs
lined the walls of the club.

In 1929, when the directors arrived, I
asked a new and uninformed secretary—
"Where is the salmon?" He replied that he had

sent it to the White House kitchen, and would get it back. He went to the kitchen to get the salmon, but found that the cook had cut off its head and tail, and otherwise prepared it for the oven. The intelligent cook was equal to the emergency. She sewed the head and tail on again and neatly stuffed it with cotton. The fish was brought out to the White House lawn. The secretary told me to hold it horizontally as it was very fragile. But one of the battery of photographers stepped up and said to me *sotto voce* that something was wrong with the fish. On hurried inspection, I found a large piece of cotton was sticking out of it.

A President must be equal to emergencies. I carefully held up the fish with my hand over the spot of cotton. The directors of the fishing club, the fish, and I posed before twenty photographers—and each posed for "just one more" six times. But the cotton kept oozing out of the fish as was proved by the later photographs. The fishing club did not use those later editions.

The Expert

Where the following story came from I do not
know. It may be apocryphal, but it contains a
point of interest to all fishermen.

I was supposed to be returning after a day's
fishing without a single fish when I met a boy
who was toting home a beautiful catch.

I asked: "Where did you get them?"

He said: "You just walk down that lane marked 'Private' till you come to a sign saying 'Trespassers Will Be Prosecuted.' Just beyond is a stream marked 'No Fishing Allowed,' and there you are."

Home Again

There are two things I can say for sure: two months after you return from a fishing expedition you will begin again to think of the snow-cap on the distant mountain peak, the glint of sunshine on the water, the excitement of the dark blue seas, and the glories of the forest.

And then you buy more tackle and more clothes for next year. There is no cure for these infections.

And that big fish never shrinks.

Composed in Monotype Bembo
by Clarke & Way, New York, New York
Printed by The Murray Printing Company,
Forge Village, Massachusetts
Bound by H. Wolff Book Manufacturing Company,
New York, New York